Animals
BIG
and
SMALL

RiverStream Readers
Animal Antonyms

by Jenna Lee Gleisner

Ideas for Parents and Teachers

RiverStream Readers let children practice reading informational texts at the earliest reading levels. Familiar words and concepts with close photo-text matches support early readers.

Before Reading
- Discuss the cover photo with the child. What does it tell him?
- Ask the child to predict what she will learn in the book.

Read the Book
- "Walk" through the book and look at the photos. Let the child ask questions.
- Read the book to the child, or have the child read independently.

After Reading
- Use the photo quiz at the end of the book to review the text.
- Prompt the child to make connections. Ask: *Are your pets big or small?*

Amicus Readers hardcover editions published by Amicus.
P.O. Box 1329, Mankato, MN 56002
www.amicuspublishing.us

Copyright © 2014. International copyright reserved in all countries. No part of this book may be reproduced in any form without written permission from the publisher.

RiverStream Publishing reprinted with permission of The Peterson Publishing Company.

Library of Congress Cataloging-in-Publication Data

Gleisner, Jenna Lee.
  Animals big and small / Jenna Lee Gleisner.
     pages cm. -- (Animal antonyms)
  Includes bibliographical references and index.
  ISBN 978-1-60753-502-7 (hard cover : alk. paper) -- ISBN 978-1-60753-530-0 (eBook)
  1. English language--Synonyms and antonyms--Juvenile literature. 2. English language--Comparison--Juvenile literature. I. Title.
  PE1591.G44 2013
  428.1--dc23

2013004328

Photo Credits: Andrey Kuzmin/Shutterstock Images, cover (top), 16 (top left); Shutterstock Images, cover (bottom left), cover (bottom right), 3 (top), 3 (bottom), 6, 7, 11, 14, 16 (top middle), 16 (bottom left), 16 (bottom middle), 16 (bottom right); Nagel Photography/Shutterstock Images, 1 (top); Dirk Ercken/Shutterstock Images, 1 (bottom); Krzysztof Odizomek/Dreamstime, 4; Prasit Chansareekorn/Shutterstock Images, 5; Vladimir Melnik/Shutterstock Images, 8; Thinkstock, 9; Geanina Bechea/Shutterstock Images, 10; Pal Teravagimov/Shutterstock Images, 12, 16 (top right); Ryan M. Bolton/Shutterstock Images, 13; Sergii Figurnyi/Shutterstock Images, 15

Produced for Amicus by The Peterson Publishing Company and Red Line Editorial.

Editor Jenna Gleisner
Designer Jake Nordby

1 2 3 4 5 CG 16 15 14 13
RiverStream Publishing--Corporate Graphics, Mankato, MN--122013--1041CGW13

Big and small are antonyms. Antonyms are words that are opposites. Which animals are big? Which animals are small?

A whale shark is big.
Whale sharks are the
biggest kind of fish.

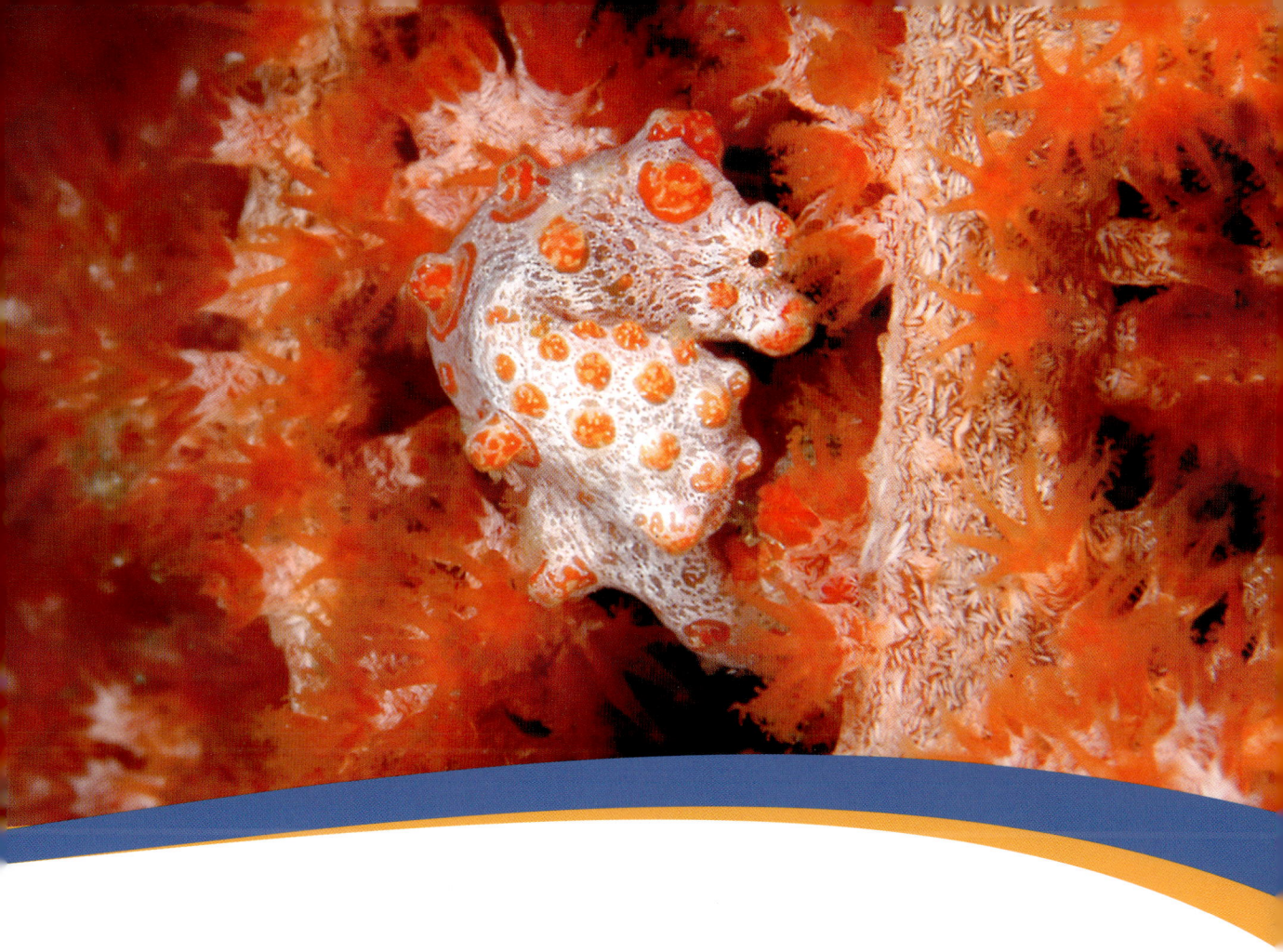

A pygmy seahorse is small. It is smaller than your finger.

A giant tortoise lives inside a big shell. The big shell protects its body.

A hermit crab is small enough to live in a seashell.

A polar bear uses its big paws to walk on snow.

A goat uses its small hooves to walk between rocks.

A toucan has a big beak.
It uses its big beak to
pluck fruit from trees.

A hummingbird has a small beak. It reaches into flowers for food.

A giraffe has big spots. The spots help it hide in tall grass.

Small spots on a salamander help it blend in with the forest floor.

What is the biggest animal you have seen?

What is the smallest?

Photo Quiz

Which animals are big?
Which animals are small?

16

Photo Quiz

Which animals are over?
Which animals are under?

16

Baby penguins cuddle
under their father's
fur to keep warm
while they sleep.

Bats wrap their wings over their faces while they sleep. They hang upside down.

Eels hide under rocks.
They wait for prey to swim by.

Pelicans fly over water to look for fish.

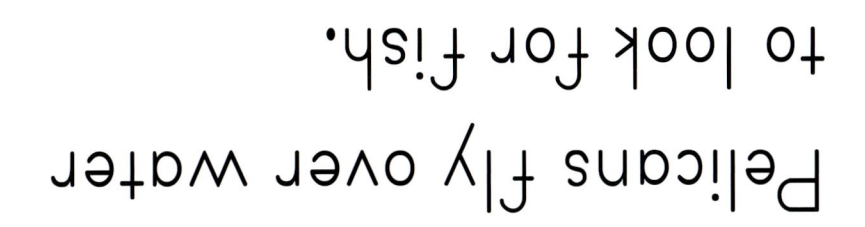

12

Stingrays swim under the water. Their large fins are connected to their heads.

Swans run over the water before they fly. They flap their wings and take off.

Moles dig tunnels under the ground to find food.

Owls fly over a field.
They spot mice to eat.

Frogs hide under leaves.
Their green color helps
them blend in.

Leopards watch over other animals from above. They hunt and sleep in trees.

Worms live under the ground. Birds pull them up with their beaks.

Giraffes can see over trees. They are the tallest animals on Earth!

Over and under are antonyms. Antonyms are words that are opposites. Which animals are over? Which are under?